Windows 10:

2019 User Manual. Everything You Need to Know About Microsoft Windows 10

Windows 10

Copyright © 2019

All rights reserved.

ISBN: 9781079056013

CONTENTS

Introduction...8

Chapter 1 – Starting with Windows 10.....................................10

    The Welcome Screen 10

    User Accounts..11

    Microsoft Account...11

    Protecting Account with a password 12

    New updates to the Start Menu..12

    Running programs and searches in the Start menu........13

    Apps to Install 14

    Start menu customization:..14

Chapter 2 – Setting up Windows 10..16

    Windows 10 Upgrade 17

    Already existing Windows 10 17

    Buying Windows 10 18

    Upgrading from Windows 7 & 8 18

Chapter 3 – Windows 10 Features...20

Windows 10

Microsoft Edge Web Browser 20

Bookmarks 21

Notes and Annotations 22

The Pen 22

Pen for Highlighter 22

Typed Notes 23

Saving Notes 23

The Reading mode 23

Page Translator 23

The more options 24

Print a Page 24

Pin a Website to the Start Menu 24

Pin Website to Taskbar 25

Change your Start Page 25

Tab Preview Bar 25

Set Aside Tabs 25

Edge Extensions 26

Connecting to the Internet with Windows 10 26

Chapter 4 – Configuration and customization of Windows 10 29

Start Menu Changes and Comparisons 29

Windows 10 Start menu and Programs 30

How to customize the Windows Start Menu and Taskbar 32

Cortana 33

Changing the Date and Time 35

Windows Desktop 35

Changing Your Desktop Background 37

Changing Display Settings 37

Changing Themes, Colors, and Sounds 37

Screen Savers 38

Windows Power Settings 39

Windows Control Panel 40

Chapter 5—The Best Windows 10 Apps 41

Adobe Photoshop express 41

VLC 42

Ninite 43

Wushowhide 44

Microsoft to-Do 44

Polarr 45

EasUS Todo Backup 45

Autoruns 46

Hotspot Shield Free VPN 47

Chapter 6—Security Tips for Windows 10 48

Update your Device 48

Limiting data Tracking 49

Avoid a Microsoft Account 50

Setting up Passwords and Sign-In Options 50

Careful with Cortana 51

Other Security Tips 52

Chapter 7—Tablet and laptop Features, also a little on Microsoft Office 53

Mobile Apps on Windows 10 54

Screen rotation in Windows 10 54

Closing Laptop Lids 54

Drawing on Sites and Switching to Tablet view 55

Virtual Desktops for More Use 56

Changing the Tablet or Laptop Location 56

About Microsoft office 57

Tips and Tricks for MS Office 58

Chapter 8—Tips and Tricks for Windows 10 61

Secret start menu 62

Adding the Desktop Button 62

Cortana Tips 62

File Explorer Sharing 63

Windows 10

Opening to This PC 63

Shake it up 64

Slide to Shutdown 64

Conclusion 66

Thank you for purchasing this book!

We always try to give more value then you expect. That's why we've updated the content and you can get it for FREE. You can get the digital version for free because you bought the print version.

The book is under the match program from Amazon. You can find how to do this using next URL: https://www.amazon.com/gp/digital/ep-landing-page

I hope it will be useful for you.

Introduction

Windows 10 is an operating system or OS, which means that it

manages the processor, memory, and drives in your machine. This is basically the hub where you run applications including your web browsers, games, and the like.

In this day and age, using a computer falls into two categories, the consumers, and creators. Creators use computers to write different media, including books and papers, and use a computer for editing photos, sites, and blogs, and it creates a desktop environment that helps them get the job done. They typically use different writing implements too, including those touchscreen pens and tablets, and so forth.

Consumers use their computers to read information, type of emails, and utilize social media and the web. They don't use it for creation, but they can. Typically, they prefer a touchscreen environment, and fortunately, Windows 10 runs well on both touchscreen devices, and regular devices to enhance the user experience.

In this, you'll learn about the different features of Windows 10, and how each of them can assist you.

Chapter 1 – Starting with Windows 10

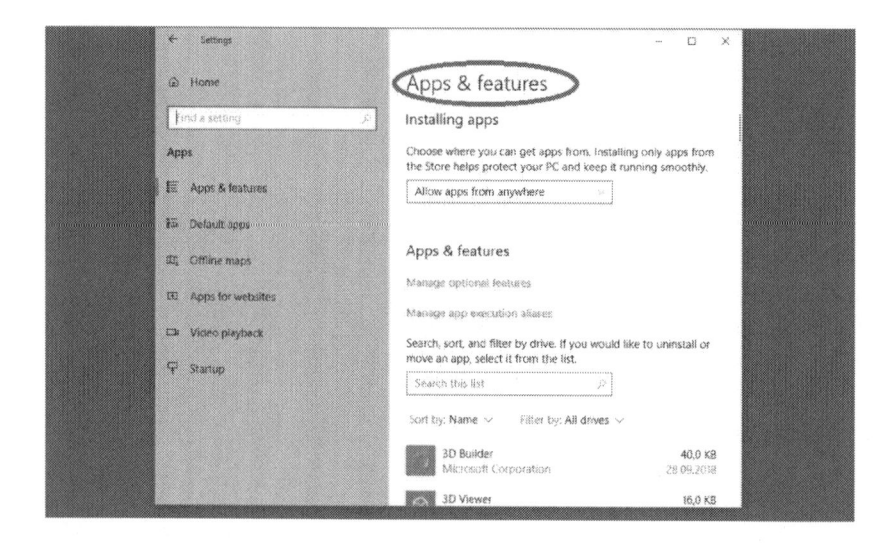

First, you have to know what you're dealing with, including the welcome screen, accounts, and the menu. That is where we'll begin with this by going through each aspect when starting Windows 10.

The Welcome Screen

This is a screen when you first turn the computer on, and usually, if you press the middle button on your machine you can go here. At this point, you get a screen that requires a password to implement, and you can personalize it. That's involves going to the start menu after logging in, going to settings, then personalization, and then the start menu, which you can toggle in order to turn on and off, and where you can determine whether you need a password as well.

User Accounts

User accounts are essentially the way to determine which desktop is whose. For example, if you have a family computer, you don't' want your kids getting into important documents, so you should let them have their own separate account.
To make these, you go to the Windows icon near the bottom, and then settings, then push the Accounts button, and then choose Family & Other users.
At this point, you can then choose to add someone to that PC. Choose the option that you don't have their information, and from there, you can have them added without a Microsoft account. If they do have one, they can just sign in, and there you go. They use the name and password they want to, and from there your'e done.
To switch users, you simply go to the upper left part of the menu in the start menu, choose the user that you want, and then they can log in. This is simple, and you can switch users easily.

Microsoft Account

You hear about these a lot, but if you plan to use Outlook, Office 365, Hotmail, Xbox, Skype, or Windows, this is what you need. It also gives you the OneDrive cloud storage on computers. Best of all, they are free and just require an email address and phone number. From here, once you have that, you can also download apps from the store, and look at device settings.

If you need one, go to www.account.microsoft.com for details.

To sign in, you push start, then settings, accounts, and then the app and email accounts, and from there, you can add a Microsoft account, add in your login details, and verify it with a code. From there, you'll be signed in, and every time you want to log in, you just choose that account, and log in from there.

Protecting Account with a password

Passwords are important for computers, naturally because there is sensitive information on them. If you are the only one using that computer, and trust those around you enough, you may not need it, but for the most part, we do need them.

How do you change the passwords though? How do you put a password in? How do you change it if you feel it has been compromised?

To put a password in, you go to accounts within the settings part of the start menu. You then go to sign-in options, and you can from there, choose to add a new password, or you can press change to change the password already there. If you change, you must sign in with the current password, and you'll need to confirm it with a confirmation code.

You will have to enter it once again to fully change it, but once that's done, that's all there is to it. You can change it to a PIN too. It is virtually the same steps, except you choose to change it into a PIN. You will need to put your old password in again, and then the PIN, but that is all that you need. PINs are much easier, but can be compromised if you are not careful.

New updates to the Start Menu

You also have new start menu updates with Windows 10 too, in order to make it more organized. The menu can be accessed at the bottom left, and you can add different folders and apps to it, in order to make it more organized. You can click on a panel, let it drop down, and then you can access whatever apps you need, including social media and utility apps. They also have a drag and drop menu too in order to make this easier for you.

Tab preview located on edge browser tells you the tabs you have opened up, and you can go through them horizontally, letting the preview bar drop down with each. There is also the option of pinning programs to the start menu, which is done with a single right-click, and choosing to pin to start. This is good for those who use certain programs a lot, and saves you time.

You also have Edge jump list, which is where you right-click the Edge icon to add a new window, making it easy to add Windows to access what you need.

The start menu also lets you organize apps into folders, allowing you to go through various apps that you have, and pinning them to these folders, making it easier to navigate and find exactly what you need.

Running programs and searches in the Start menu

Once you get to the start menu, you will have apps. To limit scrolling time, you can jump to a part of this list, allowing you to search and look for the app that you need based on the letter, and then run it. You can also type in the name into the search box, or push the Windows key and type out the app name to find this. You can then right click these in order to add or remove the programs that you want to use. Continue to pin these to start until you have what you want.

You will need to do this one by one, and if you want to add folders, libraries, files, and the like, you can with this. The newest ones are in the bottom-right corner for you to use.

Apps to Install

There are so many apps that you can install, including Instagram and Instagram stories, but some of the most popular ones include Windows Moviemaker, 8 Zip, Adobe, and media Player 5. To figure out what you need, you go to Microsoft's website, find the apps that you want, and download them. Most are free, but some may cost a little bit. However, if you do use the apps, it will be worth it, and you can always pin these new apps to start for easy access.

Start menu customization:

There is even further customization to make this better. You can re-size the menu by dragging the top of Edge with the mouse. This may increase the icon and column group utilized, and you will need to do this for up to four of these. You can also add more as you go along.

If you are running out of space, go to start, settings, and then start menu to add more tiles to the start menu.

If you have files you do not use anymore, you can always right-click them and choose to unpin to start. This is good for when you are running out of room, and it is simple if you are done with the app. You can also right-click these, resize them, and from there, you can choose what you need.

Four small tiles fit a medium, four medium to a large, and a wide one I 2 mediums, so you can choose how busy you want the screen to be.

Finally, you can turn off live-file updates by right clicking them and toggling that off. It is simple.

Windows 10

While the start menu might be complicated, after playing around with it, it is relatively easy to navigate with a bit of time.

Chapter 2 – Setting up Windows 10

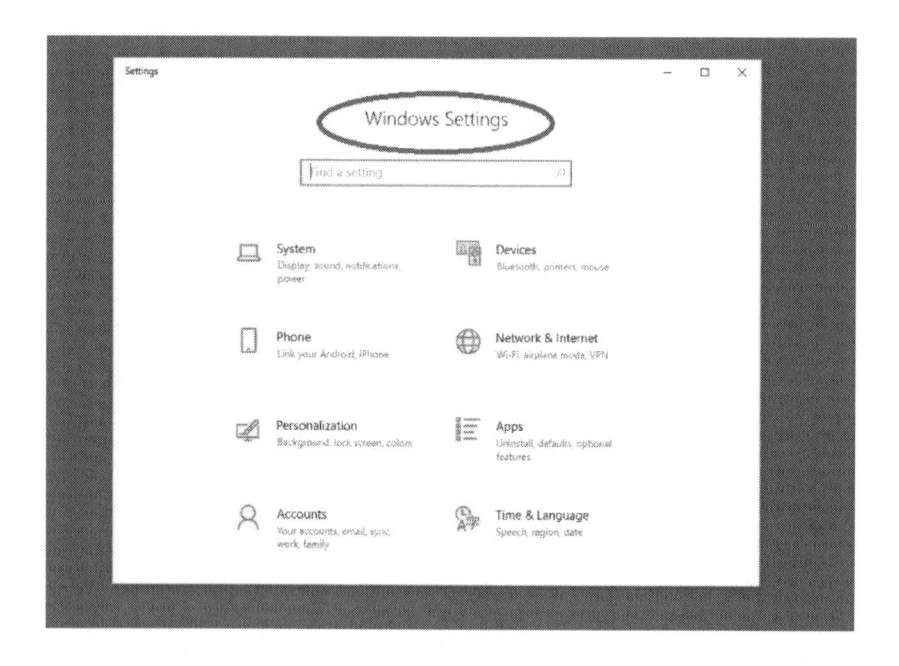

Most new devices have Windows 10 installed already, and computers that are new usually come with it. But, if you are running windows 7 or 8, you are going to need to upgrade. While the free upgrade period is over, but if you do have a Windows 7 or 8 system, there is still a free upgrade to be had. Here, we'll discuss how you can upgrade, and highlight how you can do it with the media creation tool, including installing printers, connecting to Wi-Fi, and other features that Windows 10 has to offer.

Windows 10 Upgrade

If you have a fully licensed Windows 7 or 8 machine, you can still upgrade free with a media creation tool. If you are upgrading though, you need to make sure that it has the right specs. Without it, it will run super slow. Here, we will discuss the minimum requirements you are going to need.

1 GHZ CPU or faster (ideally 2GHZ)

2 GB of RAM (4GB ideal)

20 GB of space (500 GB ideal)

800×600 screen resolution minimally

A graphics card with WDDM support, and DirectX 9 or higher support.

If you have this, you should be good to go.

Already existing Windows 10

To update Windows 10 if you already have it, you can do so usually automatically with notifications. Alternatively, you can go to start, then settings, then Apps, and then update & Security, and then Windows Update. You can check for updates at this point and download them if you have them. The 1809 October update will automatically install if you need it. It will need to restart itself, so you will want to choose to Update & Restart in the start menu. If it only says restart, wait a bit, because that means it is not fully downloaded yet.

Buying Windows 10

If you need to buy Windows 10, you ca do so online. Usually, you can get the installation media on a junk drive, DVD or a download directly from the Microsoft Online store. You can get it directly from the store, and you can choose how you want to install it. From there, you just buy and download to begin.

From there, they will take you to an order summary, and you will then need to sign in with a Microsoft account address along with a password, enter payment details and then confirm the order. You will be sent a copy if you chose to install it via a disc or USB stick. You will then get the likenesses based on your account, so if you use that Microsoft account on here, Windows will automatically activate on there, and this is good even in the event of having to re-install Windows for whatever reason.

Now, to install Windows 10 with a USB stick, you open up file explorer, go to the stick, and then go to the 'steup.exe" file. From there, you can install it.

If you do need to install via a creation tool, you will do it in a different way, and we will discuss that in the next section.

Upgrading from Windows 7 & 8

Now to begin, you need to go to www.microsoft.com/software-download/Windows10 and double click on the mediacreationtool.exe, and from there, run this. You will want to make sure that the file is in the downloads folder. Now, you will get a blue screen, and the option to upgrade the PC now. Do so, click next, and follow the instructions on the screen. Leave the setting that is selected, and from there, download and install updates, giving you the latest version, click next, and then choose to accept those terms.

You are then given a few options in the next screen, and they are as follows:

- Keep personal files, apps, and settings: this automatically transfers all of the apps, settings, and files.

- Keep personal files only: this takes out all of the old pre-installed apps, settings, and apps, but you get to keep the files. You will need to re-install everything.

- Keep nothing: you keep nothing, only do this if you have backed up everything. This gives a fresh install.

When in doubt, chose to keep everything, since it will keep all files, apps, and settings that are compatible, such as whatever you use with edge. His will keep all your files, any compatible applications and Windows settings such as Edge/Explorer, histories, themes, and whatever. From there, click next.

Windows then automatically shuts down and restarts, and from there, it will update, and setup. This does take a while so keep that in mind. You will get the Windows 10 welcome screen, and from there, choose "express settings" to keep the default settings. Click next, and from there, Windows will configure and restart. From there, you will then be on the desktop, and from there, you will have a freshly installed Windows 10 machine.

It is the same for 8, and pretty simple to do. Windows 10 is easy to install, and this section told you how.

Chapter 3 – Windows 10 Features

Windows 10 automatically comes with the Edge browser, and it has many great features, including the ability to annotate sites, share and make notes, and so much more. We'll talk a bit about Chrome and Firefox as well, and we'll also tell you about some of the other features too, including mail and calendar apps, and how this all works together to create the best experience for you as a user.

Microsoft Edge Web Browser

Edge was originally called 'Spartan" but it is known for being a lightweight browser, replacing the former Internet Explorer that used to be a part of 10. This came from the Spring Creator's Update. It is fully integrated with Cortana and OneDrive, and it also has annotation tools, modes for reading, and tools to share.

Microsoft also has a new icon for the taskbar and start menu, but here, we will talk about the edge interface, and how to navigate it...

Near the top is where the address bar is, as usual. You can also add websites to favorites, show favorites, make annotations on pages, types or written out, and do so much more b going to the toolbar near the top of the screen itself.

Bookmarks

Bookmarking is simple; you just click the star at the top. It will ask where you want to save it, and you can click the arrow near the right for options. Choose favorites to share it to a favorites list, and you can click the show favorite's icon for this. The favorite's bar of the website will show all of the sites that you ended up favorite, and you can click on these to navigate to them.

If you want to create a new favorites folder, you can go to this, and choose to "create new folder" in the field. If you want to re-examine your bookmarked sites, you can go to favorites, open up the list, and you can from there, drag the websites around to reorder them, or drag them to the yellow folders.

Yellow folders are where you can house all of the sites that are similar, properly organizing them. To create a new one, right click the favorite part, and choose to create new folder, then give it a name. You will then see the "favorites bar" underneath the edge browser, and under the address bar. It will then have three dots at the right in order to go to settings, and you can then toggle to show the favorites bar. That keeps everything neatly in one place, and allows you for proper site organizing.

Notes and Annotations

To go to annotation mode, you tap the icon in the toolbar, and you will get another toolbar that you can see. On the left-hand side, there is a pen tool, then a highlighter, and an eraser tool to get rid of annotations drawn, a note tool for typing in annotations if you cannot write them in. There is also a website snipping tool in order to copy sections of a webpage to a clipboard to put in MS word. Alternatively, note taking apps. This makes your annotating experience even better.

The Pen

The pen tool allows you to write down different things with your hands. This can also be toggled in size too for bigger or smaller notes. You can draw arrows, highlight various headings, or write text. You can also highlight a website that you find useful, and you can even send these to your favorites, and then send these to your friends as well.

Pen for Highlighter

You also have the highlighter pen to highlight different words. You can change the color with the drop-down menu, and a slider for size, and from there, you can then swipe with your finger to highlight text. In addition, an "eraser tool" can erase any highlights or annotations that you have on the page.

Typed Notes

You can also add typed notes, and its super simple. You essentially tap on the note icon, then the webpage, and where you want the note to appear. You can then add the notes with an on-screen keyboard, or an attached keyboard. This is good if you do not have the touch function for your machine.

Saving Notes

You can save and share these annotations tool, and you can get these on the right side of the toolbar. You can use the first to save, and then the second to share via email, printing, or whatever.

The Reading mode

Reading mode is available for those who have trouble reading the txt on the screen. This is good for website articles as well. Some websites also have ugly font or a background that does not work for it, so reading mode allows you to look at this in a better fashion, making utilizing the site for information even easier.

Page Translator

You can translate pages, and that is simple, and that is by going to the translate icon in the menu. In the drop-down box, Edge will detect the language and then go to the from field, and from there in the to field, choose the language you want to translate, which is perfect for pages not in your own language, allowing you to use them as needed.

The more options

There are even more options in edge, and they are available in the

Windows 10

settings menu. Those are the three dots, from there, you can access a whole bunch of other features, including printing the page, make it bigger, the zoom function, and from there, sharing the current web page through social media with the share feature. There is also the find feature here, which allows you to find the keywords by typing them in. You can also print the page, adjust the settings and security, and enhance your privacy here too.

Print a Page

Printing pages allows you to print them out, and this is the first of the options in the three dots area. If you click this, it gives you a dialogue box asking for where to print it out. You can print in portrait or landscape, and in color or black and white. From here, you can look at the preview, and then print when you think it is ready to go.

Pin a Website to the Start Menu

You can also pin websites to the start menu, a useful feature to use. You essentially open the Edge website, and from there go to the three dots icon that is on the right side of where the window is.

From here, you go to the drop-down menu, and then choose to pin this to start. Choose yes when prompted with whether you should pin this to start. You can then access the page directly from the start menu. You can find it there, and it usually has the Edge loco underneath it.

Pin Website to Taskbar

You can also do this with websites, and it is good for sites you visit a lot. Do not use this too much because you will fill up the taskbar with all these sites, making it a nightmare to navigate.

Do this, open up the site that you want to pin to Edge, and then you will see it, usually with the icon that the site has.

Change your Start Page

You can also change the start page if you want to, especially if you like to go to Google search for what you need. Internet Explorer did not have this, but Edge does. To change it, go to more options, and then choose settings. You can then go down to the drop-down menu, and choose a specific start page to begin with. You can then type in the web address, such as Google to begin with when you open up edge.

Tab Preview Bar

Tab preview tells you what is open on the webpage itself. To preview this, go to tab preview on the list and from there, expand on this to give a preview of the currently open tabs and then click to switch to there.

Set Aside Tabs

Edge browser uses tabs, allowing you to set aside what you need to open, to use later. This helps to avoid the visual clutter if you have many tabs. To set these aside, go to the left of the screen and choose to set aside on there. You will see all of the open websites disappear, and a new blank shows up. It literally sets these aside to look at them later on, which helps. To view the tabs that you have, you go to the left icon, and then you can see the thumbnail previews of these sites, and then click to go back there. As always, you can then click the three dots, and then share the tabs via email or social media, or add to favorites.

Edge Extensions

You can now get extensions on the edge browser.

In order to get these, you go to the three dots, and then choose extensions. From the sidebar, you can see the installed extensions. You can then choose to get extensions from the store. While there are only a few extensions currently, the list is growing over time. These extensions can be accessed at any time, and that is by going to more, and then going to extensions.

You can actually change the settings by clicking on the name, and you can disable and enable extensions in the options menu. You also can see webpages and preferences that is there, and uninstall these extensions too.

Connecting to the Internet with Windows 10

For those who are just coming through with a new system for setting up their connection with Windows 10, it is important to make sure that you have a stable and set internet connection. You should understand that Windows 10 has many different ways to connect to the internet, and here, we will talk about how you can do that.

There is one way to do it, and it is via the action center. You literally can do this by clicking on it in the bottom right corner, or just by pressing the Windows key and then A. From there, you then want to go to wireless in the quick actions section. You will

Windows 10

then see all of the different Wi-Fi networks that are available to you. From there, you choose the wireless network to connect to, and it will either connect you automatically, or ask for your password or network security key, which you can do in the next screen.

There is also connecting manually. You may want to not have your computer connect automatically for a variety of reasons. While an automatic connection does work, you may not want to connect it automatically for the sole reason of you do not want to be distracted, would like to save battery, and the like. But of course, even when no connected, the Wi-Fi network will look for networks, taking your battery. While Windows 10 offers the chance for you to connect automatically, if you want to have a manual option, you can do that. First, you go to the wireless icon near the bottom right, and then tap it to turn the Wi-Fi off. It will also reveal a setting where you can chooses to turn it back on. You also can choose to turn on the Wi-Fi manually, and set it for a certain time. It can be an hour, to four hours, to one day, and then you choose the manual option. When you want to connect this to the internet, from there turn it back on, and choose the network to join. From there, it will automatically connect to a system in which the adapter will connect and configure. If you do decide to connect to a Wi-Fi network, you totally can as well in this too.

Finally, you have setting up the broadband connection, which allows you to connect multiple computers to their network. Windows 10 has this. Now, to start this, you go to settings, and then network and internet, and then dial-up, and from there, choose to start a new connection. From there, it will launch the setup for this connection wizard, and it works well with computers that are connected via Ethernet. You can choose to connect to the internet, and then broadband, and from there, you then enter the username, ISP, and the password in order to connect it. You then will want to select whom you share the connection to, allowing those users to connect as well, and you may have a shared DNS IP address, and you can set those in the network adapter. When you set it up, you should use the router, it will help when you have multiple computers that require this type of connection.

And there you have it, all about connecting to the internet, and why it matters, and how Windows 10 allows you to do that, and so much more.

Edge is better than ever, and here, we discussed how you can reap the full benefits of Edge as well.

Chapter 4 – Configuration and customization of Windows 10

In this chapter, we will be diving deeper into Windows 10 configuration and customization. There is a lot to do, and we will show you how you can achieve all of this.

Start Menu Changes and Comparisons

The first thing you will notice in terms of changes when compared to Windows 7 and 8, is that 10 has a different start menu. The menu in 7was great, and easy to use. This one gets more to the

Windows 10

point, and you can find all of the different utilities that you need to find.

Windows 8 did not even have start menu, but in the 8.1 update, they brought it back, but the menu was definitely not that pretty, and the 'tile" interface definitely didn't work for computer users. Windows 10 essentially combined both the Windows 8 and 8 menus to create the best popup start menu with customizable tiles possible. There are other differences as well; including security, improvements and the Windows apps and Microsoft store, but that is the gist of what your'e getting.

Windows 10 Start menu and Programs

Now that you have upgraded, it is time to discuss how this all works. You need to understand that there are multiple ways to do the same thing, so figure out what is best for you, and use that method. Do not worry about the rest.

It is a bit of a learning curve for everybody, but you should focus on two areas. The first is to find the programs.

You can add program shortcuts. You can also called icons, in different places, including the desktop, or the taskbar, but once you click on them, they essentially do the same thing as before.

Let us talk about Windows 7 again. When you clicked on the start button, you saw all the programs that were there. With Windows 10, it is not the case, it mostly just shows specific and most recently used apps and programs.

There is a method to see everything though, and if you want to, you go to the search box and type in %app data%\Microsoft\Start Menu and then press enter. After that, you will get a dialogue box showing you the programs, and from there, you right click the folder, choose properties, and from there check the box that says hidden, and click apply.

You can then apply changes to the subfolder, and press okay, and you will apply changes to the folder and sub-folders and from there, you can simply press okay.

Now what should happen is you should see the missing programs, and from there, when you click the start button, it will all be there.

Now, we can talk about finding the installed programs. From here, all of the programs should be listed, but you can also get them via shortcuts on the desktop or taskbar, which is next to the start button, and is where the click is. You can add or remove shortcuts as needed, and a good rule of thumb is usually, less is more, so do not clutter this too much. You can also copy and paste these shortcuts in order to help you organize everything you need in a singular place.

Finally, you need to know where your files are, and file management allows you to copy/paste, move, delete, or whatever you Ned with your files. This can help you find what you need for a job that your'e interested in, or you want to copy photos to the computer. If you know how to browse the file and copy it to the phone, you will be able to find everything that you need. If you do not have this, you are going to have a lot of trouble finding what you need.

You can go to file explorer to help you find all of the files, and there is a search function to find what you need. You should look into this, and you can access it via the start menu, taskbar, or searching for this. Knowing this will help make tasks much easier for you, and less overwhelming.

How to customize the Windows Start Menu and Taskbar

Here, we will talk about how to customize both the start menu and taskbar, in order to help you find all that you need. You can customize this in many different ways, such as an alphabetical listing from left to right, or even grouping these together in order to "pin" these to the start menu. You can put them in groups, and rename and customize these too.

By right clicking on an item on the left, you can always remove it from the start menu, and you can do other functions including running the program as a local administrator, or uninstalling this. If you right-click an item, you also can unpin it from the start menu, pin to the taskbar, uninstall it, and the like. There might be other options depending on the program. To make a custom group for this, you drag an existing tile to the top or button of the start menu area, automatically creating a new group for this. From there, you can add or remove the tiles as you need, and you can choose the drag and drop options from other groups to the left of this, rearranging the other items from the groups in order to organize these by preference. If you go to settings and click on personalization, and then start, you will have many other options.

Some of these include making the screen full screen, showing only recent items, and so on. At this point, you can also choose which folders you want to show on the start menu too, including documents, pictures, and the like. It also can show any recent suggestions and opened folders too.

You should remember that with Windows 10, is that Microsoft is changing things, so make sure that you learn this, so that the next change is not too much to deal with.

You can also customize the taskbar, including switching from default view, combining the taskbar buttons, and so forth, enhancing thee experience. When you open up programs, they take up space, but this allows you to switch these around, and when you close the program, it will automatically be removed, unless it is pinned to the taskbar.

Combining the taskbar allows the icons to be smaller, and

combines them, which is great for grouping them together, and you can see side-by-side previews on what you want.

There is also the never combine option, which if you do not do that, it will never combine these together, which makes it easy to see, but takes up a lot of space. If you do have a larger monitor with a decent screen resolution, this will not be an issue though. If you like this, but want to save space, choose the use small taskbar buttons in settings.

Taskbar settings can be found in the personalization area of Windows 10. It also includes other options including locking the taskbar so it's not hidden or moved, giving you more space, and a setting to put the taskbar on the side or top of the screen, so you can play with this and determine what's best for you.

Cortana

Cortana is basically the Siri of Windows devices, and you can use this to set reminders, make lists, or search for information on the web, and apps. When you configure Windows for the first time, they will ask if you want to use Cortana. You can always choose to use it later on if you say no. It will be put in the taskbar next to the start menu, and you can type in general searches here too. You also have the option to put this as an icon to perform searches, or hide it, which saves desktop space. You can change this by right clicking on a blank part of the taskbar, and then choose the Cortana option.

You can change many different settings with Cortana, and some settings you can configure include:

- Setting up a mic to use Cortana with
- Changing the default language

- Shortcuts for the keyboard.

- Changing search settings from strict, to either moderate or off

- Turning the history on or off

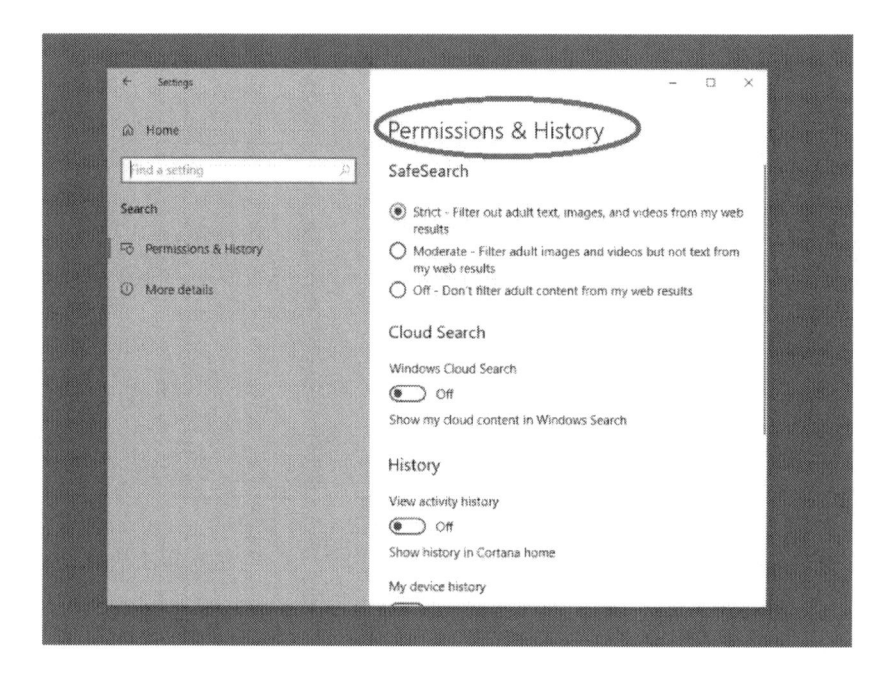

- Notification options

- Enabling Cloud Search

Cortana can do a lot, and it might be something worth using if needed.

Windows 10

Changing the Date and Time

One thing that you will want to know as well is changing the date and time settings as needed. You may need to do this if you install it and the date and time settings aren't correct. It might be because of an improper time zone being set, or the BIOS clock is off. You also may need to adjust the motherboard, but that is something that may require a more detailed fix, since that typically doesn't fix itself completely. To fix that, it depends on the motherboard and manufacturer, abut if you see a prompt before you start Windows, you can press either F2 or Del to go to BIOS and check this

BIOS is a menu system that uses arrow keys or numbers. If it is just a case of an incorrect time zone, you just right click on the clock in order to adjust the date and time. Depending on the version of this, the configuration does vary, but once there, you can choose what you need to see, and there is a drop-down menu with other options.

If the "change date and time" button is in gray, which means that it has the 'set time automatically" option turned on. So you will want to turn this off, and then you can change it. There is also an automatic daylight savings time function that you can toggle as needed.

Windows Desktop

At this point, we'll discuss how you can navigate the desktop effectively to create a better experience.

File and folder creation

Windows 10 lets you customize the Windows desktop. The desktop is a term that shows the main screen where you have your programs, files, and folders that you use. It is essentially what your monitor sits on top of, and is an overview of everything that you

Windows 10

need to work with this. This is extremely customizable though, and you can add shortcuts, programs, or whatever, so long as it can be added.

You can add files and folders of any type on there, and if you right click on the blank part of the desktop and choose new, you'll have multiple options for items to add to there. You will want to choose one of the different options that you are given, this does vary in choice, and it will make it look different.

Creating new folders, shortcuts, contacts, and word documents is all possible, and you can customize what you see on the menu itself.

Let us take an example, the Microsoft word document. After you click on this, it will create the file on the desktop, and enable you to name it what you wish. After that, as you open the document, it will be blank, because it is a new file. You can get the same results by clicking MS Word from the start menu programs, coming up with the document, and then saving it there. When you do, you will notice it is all there, making it easier for you to find what you need.

If you want to copy a file to the desktop, it is simple, you just find the folder or file, right click it, copy, and then right click on desktop to paste this. You can also find this, and from there copy it to the desktop. You can do this with a CD/DVD or external flash.

If you open up the File\Windows explorer, there is a shortcut to the desktop on the upper left side, and you will notice how the items match what is on the desktop. Another useful way is to find it under the user's folder in the drive, which is usually the C drive. You can navigate to C:\Users\Name of drive\desktop, where it is and then log onto there. If you have other user accounts, you can go to the desktops as well, assuming you have permissions on the computer to do so.

Windows 10

Changing Your Desktop Background

You can also change the desktop. Background, and while there are many images you can choose, you can also find one from a website. To change this, you right click part of the desktop background, go to the personalize option, and once there, you can go to the personalization and background settings, allowing you to have the option to make the picture either be a solid color, or a slideshow. The slideshow option will change the image using pictures from folders of your choosing. You can also browse to find pictures that you have stored on the hard drive. Choosing the fit setting can allow you to choose how it will be displayed, whether fill, stretch, fit, tile, or whatever.

Changing Display Settings

Another thing to change is the display settings, and you can access this by right clicking an area and going there, or just going to system in settings. This allows you to change the resolution for better picture quality. While there is a recommended setting, you do not have to use this. You can also change the text size, and apps needed to enlarge them to make them easier to look at. If you have a monitor that rotates, you can go between portrait and landscape modes, and you can change seeing under orientation. If you are the type that likes to have multiple monitors, you can change that and set up multiple displays here too.

Changing Themes, Colors, and Sounds

You can also change the Windows theme, color, and sounds. The theme is the settings that include the image, colors, sounds, and cursor options. Windows 10 has some built-in themes that you can try, or download more from the Microsoft store. You can even get custom themes created so you can go back to it later if you want to change it.

Themes are found under personalization, and then themes. If you want to change the sounds and colors used, you can do it from personalization as well. There is no option for sounds other than the themes section, and that is because it still uses the older control panel interface, so you can access the sound settings there. Once you open up the sound options, you'll see its set to the Windows default sound. Under program events, you can change the sound for events, including when Windows starts up, and when you connect a usb device, or there is a system error. You can use the Windows sounds, WAVE files they're called, if you find some. If you don't want specific sounds, you don't have to use that.

Screen Savers

You can add these to Windows 10 as well, and the interface is the same one used since the beginning for the most part. You can go to personalization and choose this, and you can choose what you want. Depending on what you choose, the settings button can further customize it.

Windows 10

Windows Power Settings

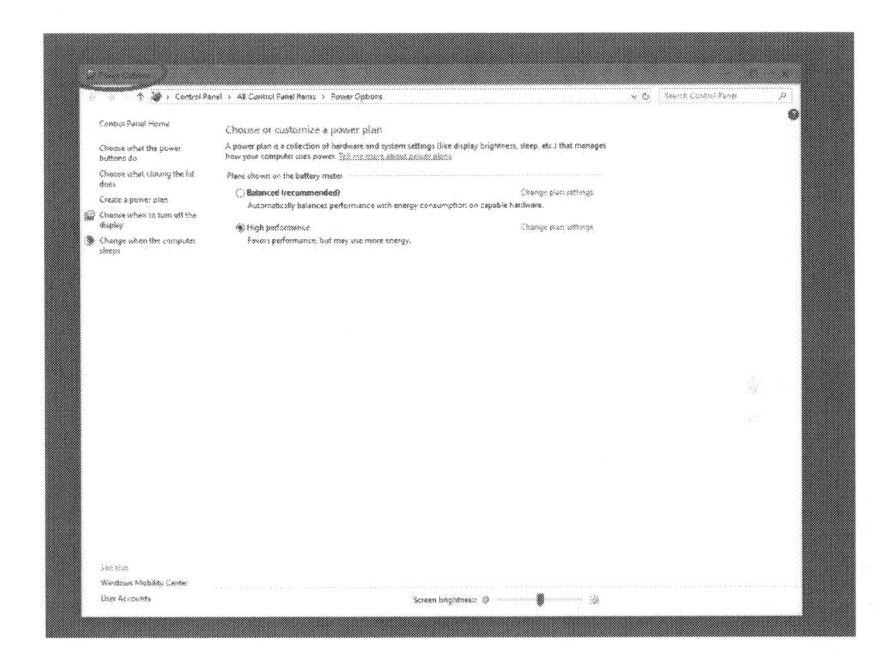

Then there are the power settings, which determines whether a computer is hibernating or sleeping after a bit, or to turn off the hard drive or monitor after a while. Sleep mode saves open files and settings in memory, and puts the computer into a low power mode. Hibernate saves the files to the disc, and turns off the computer. As you move or click the mouse or keys, you can wake it up, and it'll be the same way as left before. However, the one downside is that it takes a bit to wake it up, and sometimes it may not do so at all, so it will need to be rebooted.

You can turn off the display option, so that when you walk away for a bit, the monitor will power off, but it's the monitor alone, and when you click the mouse, it turns it back on. There are other power settings to configure too, including turn off the hard disk after a bit to save power. Our computers are pretty energy-efficient today, so you could probably keep things running without draining it too much.

If you are running a laptop that uses battery power, you may want to consider these features. In the Windows 10 settings under system, there is a power and sleep section, which lets you configure all of the different options for when you choose to turn off the system and put it to sleep. However, you will need to change the more advanced settings in control panel. This lets you choose preconfigured plans, and you can change these settings like that. You can also change the advanced power settings link to get advanced options.

At the top of this there is a drop-down menu where you can choose the power plan, and then customize it. If you want to change things to default, you click Restore Defaults to do it.

Windows Control Panel

For serious Windows users, you will want to get familiar with the control panel, which is where you can go to fix the configuration settings and options in order to change how it operates, or to fix the problems you run into. Many of the settings can be done via Windows 10 settings, but some you'll need to go to control panel specifically for ease.

You can get to this by typing in control panel in the search menu or Cortana. If it's the first time opening this, you'll see the category display view, but if you click the down area by view by, you can change the icons for it to be larger and smaller.

There are so many settings in Windows, but if you take some time and understand these features, you'll be quite amazed at what this can do, and the benefits of this as well.

Chapter 5—The Best Windows 10 Apps

We touched a little bit, on what you can get with Windows 10, but here, let's dive into the best Windows 10 apps that you can get for your device, and why they are the best out there.

Adobe Photoshop express

What is this, a Photoshop that is free? Yes, the Adobe Photoshop express is a little bit of a watered-down version of the popular photo editing system, which lets you optimize your photos with just a few presses. There is actually a selection of different "looks" which you can choose, and these are kind of like Instagram filters, but there are actually more options, especially for images. For example, if you need to smooth out your skin, this is actually one of the ways to do it. There are also different ways to bring out the blues and the greens of landscapes. You can crop, flip, straighten, and adjust the exposure and color of this. You can also fix red eye and blemishes, and there is even an auto enhance tool. You will not have to worry about paywalls, and the only payoff of this is you need to create either an Adobe ID, or just log in with a Google or Facebook account. But, it's a great free system for those looking for alternatives that fit what they need.

VLC

This is a media player that's available for practically every device out there, and this is probably the one media player that you want. It's now available for mobile devices, but also Xbox, and HoloLens too. It's pretty much compatible with every single media type out there, without the additional plugins and the codecs that you may need. When you first launch it, it will detect the connected storage, and from there, offer for you to use this media library to copy the media from the Windows 10 device's internal storage. From there, the controls are simple, and it is possible to lock them, so you don't skip any scenes either. The one in the Microsoft store doesn't support Blu-ray and DVD playback, but you can get pretty much any other media off of this, making it even better than other media players out there.

Windows 10

Ninite

If you are looking for the one-stop location for all of your desktop applications, then you'll want this. You can click on the applications you desire, and Ninite will download the latest one, free of crap ware that could be on there, and from there, it's all on there. It supports over 87 different Windows programs, and the beauty of this is that each app is a click away, without the fuss and nags, and no extra charge. You can have this update and install all of the newest machines in minutes. It misses a few of the favorites, but this is still one of the best, and you can use Secuna to help ensure that all of the latest programs are up to date. There are pro versions of this too for more of what you want from this. You can also manually run the free Ninite anytime, and the latest versions, and Ninite even proactively watches your installed programs. It's one of the best apps for Windows 10, and best of all, it's mostly free.

Wushowhide

Unless you have a corporate network and a managed update server, you may get all of the packages based on Microsoft's schedule, and you can keep the reboot limited to when you're working, but the patches happen whenever they are available. Plus, if you uninstall a patch, every time you reboot or log in again, the same patch comes in. But, this is actually a way to help you block these updates, and this is actually a way to block these updates. You can manually choose to hide or allow these updates, and you definitely can prevent these from coming in if you don't want to dal with the drama of updates, and forced updates causing a mayhem. This prevents that, making it easy for you.

Microsoft to-Do

If you want task management, you'll realize that with this, there is no shortage, but this is a hard one to beat. It's super simple, and it involves just creating a master list of these deadlines, and choose which ones you want to complete today. The current tasks that are happening today appear under the «my day» section, and from there, they can be set to disappear once they are finished. It's like Trello, but it alerts you assign the work to different people as well, and it also lets you do more everyday tasks and it can even be used to post birthday cards, buy items, or even just project management, and you can share this with others too, making this easily and readily available for you to use.

Polarr

This is a photo editing app, and if you know how to edit photos and such on your phone, you may already know about this one. This is a powerful free photo editor available for Windows 10, and it gives you two different interface options, both express, and pro as well. Both are great with the touchscreen and mouse, but the primary difference is that the icons in the pro version are not labelled, so you can have more room for images as well. It's perfect for those who want to have a good photo editing software, and it does detect the face automatically, and will help apply the skin smoothing, filters, and different dividers and texts. It's a shame that some of the options, such as overlays and such, are only available to those premium users, but the free edition is great for this, and it allows for you to enhance your photos and make a lot of great changes to this. It's worth checking out for those who use Windows 10 devices.

EasUS Todo Backup

Backing up your information is important, and it will allow you to restore function. Windows 8.1 threw this away, and Windows 7 had a decent system, but 10 has it, but it's not that good. The way to do this is you need to type in backup in the search box. They want you to stick everything into onedrive, and from there, use the refresh/restore points on there, but people don't like that for many reasons, ranging from issues with privacy, to the stupid requirements that this requires fro any of the non-Microsoft programs and media. For example, if you want to have something on there, you need to make sure you have the media on there, and there are lots of backup programs that are better for you to use. EaseUS Todo Backup is one of the best, and it's actually a really good free installation. You can back everything up, creating full disks, and you can have it back up everything, and it runs these backups once a week, for every 30 or so minutes. You won't get the outlook backups unless you pay for them, but it's still pretty good.

Autoruns

Then there is Autoruns, which is a very fast auto starting program that you have going on. This includes drivers, codecs, shell extensions, or whatever it might be, in every single obscure place. It lists these programs, telling you what you should turn off, and it does have some minor features, including the ability to filter out the Microsoft-signed programs, and allow you to jump the folders that hold the auto starting programs, and a command=-line version that lets you display the file hashes. Autoruns doesn't require installation, but instead, it runs, collects the information, and from there, it will fade away once you're done with it. It's totally free, and is a great option for anyone.

Hotspot Shield Free VPN

Finally, there is hotspot Shield Free VPN, which is one of the few free VPN options that is available, and it's actually a trusted VPN. While most of the time you do need to pay for these, this one doesn't require you to do it. They will prompt you to pay for a premium subscription, or start a seven-day free trail, but if you tap the back arrow, you can use this, and from there, you can tap connect, and get a virtual IP address. It's super simple to utilize, and while the free vision isn't good for streaming, it's good for circumventing censorship, and allows you to access any region-locked content that's there. It only has a 500MB download limit, and it also has come under fire since it may use the data to create targeted ads, but the developer does deny it. But, if you want a quick and dirty free VPN that works well, this is probably one of the best options that's out there currently, and it allows for you to create the best experience possible.

These free options are pretty good for you to try out, and there are so many different means that you can try out, and you'll be able to easily create a nice and friendly atmosphere for this. There is a lot that you can get out of these apps, and these are some of the best for what you may need.

Chapter 6—Security Tips for Windows 10

Security is a big part of Windows 10. If you know this, you'll definitely want to make sure you have the best security possible. Here, we'll discuss the top security tips for your Windows 10 experience.

Update your Device

For the most part, you should always keep your Windows system up to date, and usually, Windows does these updates automatically, but the reality of it is, for the most part lots of people don't like to deal with these updates, and sometimes they delay them. With the newest update,

Windows 10

you can completely turn these off, which might seem great, but the truth is, this doesn't fix the security issues, and in turn, it can make everything much worse for you. So, you will want to make sure that, you do update every now and then. You can always look to see if your'e getting them by going to settings, then update and security, then Windows update, and then advanced options, and look at the settings there.

Additionally, you will want to make sure that your security software is up to date. Windows 10 comes with basic protection for malware, but if you want a more complete version, you should make sure that you do purchase or invest in some sort of software. This will in turn prevent it from being hit with attacks from malware, and other ransom ware issues, including security, and other banking protections that help, and you can usually put this on multiple devices, especially if you tend to worry about this a lot.

Limiting data Tracking

This is another important element to put in. You should always go to your privacy settings, by hitting start and going to settings, then privacy, and from there, you will want to go to feedback and diagnostics, and change the feedback frequency to never. You should use a basic setting when it comes to diagnostic and usage data, and with these settings in place, you can reduce the data that's gathered from your camera, location, microphone, and the like.

Also as an aside, you should make sure that you limit the data that your'e sending to Microsoft, and if you're using Edge, you should definitely turn this off. You will want to go to the ellipsis symbol in the edge browser, choose advanced settings, and from there, go to privacy and services. You will then see options that say "have Cortana assist me with edge." turn that off. You should also stop the page prediction as well, by toggling that to off. It is a good way to amp up your security in many different cases.

Avoid a Microsoft Account

But wait, isn't that supposed to be the way to get all of the features? While, yes, that is the case, you probably won't want to use a Microsoft account. From a security point, you can keep your information and activity to a local computer, but the thing is, you can avoid the potential security issues that come with this. From a security point of view, the Microsoft account that you're using is providing programs, and services in a backend way, and they can use that to monitor information that you utilize, day in and day out. So, while yes this can be convenient to have your Outlook files and your OneDrive account there, there is the security risks here.

Setting up Passwords and Sign-In Options

If you haven't already set up a password, you should definitely do this. While you may not use a login password with Windows, without one, you're essentially leaving your computer vulnerable to anyone who grabs it, and you should never leave it anywhere by accident, because that is a good way to get completely ruined by that. The best way to prevent this is to go to settings, then account, and then sign-in options. You should, underneath password, choose to add, and from here, follow the steps that are there. You can use a Microsoft account too, but remember what we just said about those, so you may not want to do that. Without a way to sign-in, you are putting yourself in danger, but the thing is, Microsoft can also track your activity a lot more, so be careful with this. But, do choose a username and password, making it strong and long, and include both upper and lower case characters, along with punctuation too in order to ensure that you have a nice security system in place.

Additionally, you may want to consider other sign-in options. There is the Dynamic Lock, which lets you pair your smartphone to your computer via bluetooth, so you can automatically lock the computer with your smartphone within range. Might be a good idea. There is also the Windows Hello and other biometric features you can use. If your computer supports facial recognition, this might be a great option, but again, also does bring forth that potential for security breaches and people storing that information. You have sign-in options, and you should consider other sign-in options rather than just a password, especially if your'e worried about anything being compromised.

Careful with Cortana

Cortana might seem like the perfect thing to have on hand. After all, you've got all of this information, a smart assistant that's actually well, smart, and someone that can help you with whatever you need. Sounds perfect, right? Well, it's the perfect recipe for disaster if your'e not careful. It can be incredibly intrusive, especially since Cortana is always gathering information on what you do with the computer. That is to personalize your experience and it definitely may give you 1984 vibes, and not in a good way. Plus, what's even worse is your Cortana data is stored on a cloud, it can definitely be nan incentive to minimize the data sent. You can go to settings, Cortana, and search, and with the newest updates, you can separate the search bar so that you're not having to worry about Cortana getting a little too personal with your information.

Other Security Tips

There are a few other security types that can help you. For example, you should turn off advertising ID, turn on the smartscreen filter to check the content, turn off the information that's sent to Microsoft period, and make sure that you don't let apps on your devices open up apps, or let apps on your other devices use Bluetooth, since this can potentially leave you open to threats. You should also make sure that you don't get personalized ads, or control these. You probably may not want any of these. You should also turnoff all of the location information, and do it for apps specifically. You should also turn off the speech, inking, and typing, because while it does help Windows and Cortana help understand you, it leaves you open for attacks.

All of these are important to understand, and you should know by now that there are some better ways to protect yourself rather than rely on the security software that Windows provides.

Chapter 7—Tablet and laptop Features, also a little on Microsoft Office

Being a tablet and laptop owner is quite nice, and if you've been curious about getting Windows 10 for this, there are features that you can benefit from. Here are some tips for this, and here, we'll also touch a little bit on Microsoft office as well, and why it matters.

Mobile Apps on Windows 10

With the new Windows 10, a lot of the "universal apps" that are on this, do work on mobile devices, including the Windows phone, and the iOS. Though it does depend on what the developers that are taking advantage of this feature want to port to this, it means less disconnect between the mobile and desktop, and if you have a tablet, nowadays, you can actually connect this straight to the desktop for more connectivity and more fun.

Screen rotation in Windows 10

Screen rotation is something that a lot of tablets have. Usually, if you pick them up, they automatically rotate, turning it vertically and horizontally. It is good to have autorotation, but if you do have it happen unexpectedly, it can be super annoying. Most of these tablets, even with Windows 10, come with a rotation lock against the edge. Pressing that button works to keep it in place. You can always go from the start screen and check the desktop tile, right clicking a blank part of the background, choosing screen irresolution, and then check the box that allows for auto rotation, and if you check this it will rotate. If you don't, it will not rotate nearly as much, staying in place as you move this.

Closing Laptop Lids

But wait, doesn't it just turn off? Well, usually, it may not do that, and you can toggle how your laptop behaves when you latch the lid. You go to the right bottom corner, and choose control panel. Go to system and security, and from there, power options, and then choose what closing the lid does to the left pane. Windows offers three options for this, whether they be do nothing, hibernate, or shut down. You can choose how this behaves.

Typically your laptop will slumber in low power, and it will wake up without delay. But, you'll want to power off if your'e done using this, letting it conserve the battery, and wake itself up to be fully charged.

Drawing on Sites and Switching to Tablet view

This is a new feature for those who have computers that have the stylus-enabled laptops or tablets. Touchscreen PCs do this as well. You can actually take advantage of this, and you can draw on these sites. It also allows for you to have distraction-free views and other list features, allowing you to write or draw directly on these web pages, and share this with others. It's a great way to really enhance your computer experience.

In addition, if you have Windows 10 continuum, it's a new feature that you can automatically switch from the desktop to the tablet view if you have those 2-in-1 PCs, such as the Microsoft surface. When you disconnect from the keyboard, Windows will them prompt you to have tablet view, which gives you an interface that focuses on touch, larger menus, and a task bar that is easy to touch. Tablet mode is good for tapping, and you can always manually switch to tablet mode from Windows 10 and the action center in the taskbar. This was one of the features that was announced a while back, but it is a great way to enhance the integration between a smooth desktop, and a tablet mode as well.

Virtual Desktops for More Use

This is a feature that those who use tablets should take advantage of, especially if you're working with limited screen and real estate. Many of us do have multiple Windows that are there throughout the day, and this can be really annoying to deal with. Virtual desktops, which can be used, allow you to organize your apps into different views of the desktop, allowing for you to use additional workspaces in order to move these apps around, and from there, you can choose task view from the taskbar, and then drag the app to the desktop, and you can choose where it should be shown. While virtual desktops aren't new, for those who are working in a table environment will benefit immensely from this.

Changing the Tablet or Laptop Location

The joys of a tablet are that they usually don't adjust to the location. While some of them do change with the wifi, not all of them do, and you should make sure that you know exactly where you can change the time zone and location. On a tablet, you click the clock there, change the date and time, and select the time zone from the list, and choose okay. It's pretty simple and just like a regular PC and there is actually an Additional Clocks feature, which allows you to add a second clock, and let you check the time quickly, which is really nice if you're looking to stay on top of this.

This is definitely a good thing to have, and while we've touched mostly a lot of the features that are available to tablets and laptops, we haven't discussed Microsoft office, and the features of this, and we will below.

About Microsoft office

Microsoft office is essentially the software that is used to help do different actions. They include Microsoft word, Excel, PowerPoint, and Outlook. Word is a word processor, Excel is essentially a spreadsheet system, PowerPoint is used for presentations, and Outlook is the email services, and it is used to essentially do different tasks. Microsoft office does some with the OneDrive as well, which is a cloud drive where you can store all of your information, and it is pretty easy to navigate. It does use a subscription service in order to do this, and users get free updates to everything.

there are many other different components to this as well, including Microsoft publisher, which is used for making brochures, labels, calendars, business cars, newsletters, sites, and cards. There is also Microsoft access that allows you to create a database system, and has some graphical along with different software tools that come with this. There is also One-Note, which is used to help take notes, both handwritten and typed, and also comes with clippings from screens and commentates. With OneNote, you can essentially put notes for just about everything that is included in this, and it is essentially a part of Microsoft office now, being a system that's existed since 2003 but wasn't a part of MS Office till 2013.

Finally, there is also Skype for business, which allows you to communicate with others, and host conferences in real time. It's a communication app, and it allows for you to have a good network. It is pretty good.

while there are also other different aspects that are good for business, there are actually two mobile apps that are now a part of Microsoft office, and they are office lens, which is an image scanner optimized for mobile devices, capturing the document via the camera, straightening it up, and you can then upload it to of word, OneNote, powerpoint, or even outlook or just save it to OneDrive, and it'll be stored there. It's quite helpful.

There is also office remote, which turns mobile devices into a remote control to control the desktop versions of word, excel, and powerpoint too, creating a more interesting ecosystem than before.

Tips and Tricks for MS Office

Here, we'll discuss a few tips that you can use with MS Office.

To start, if you feel overwhelmed by your inbox, you can go to the inbox, then home, and then clean up, and you can clean all of the different redundant, and read messes to deleted items. It will never remove unread messages, and this can help to clear everything away easily.

You can also add signatures to your messages, and you can go to the email message, then signature, and choose signatures. By choosing new, you can give your signature a name, and create a signature. You can add different links and graphics, getting creative with fonts and different colors, and you can push okay to start using this. This is a great way to answer your personal messages.

Windows 10

You also can clear your formatting in a document. You can copy something from elsewhere but you don't want to change the font on this, you can copy it, and then press control, then shift, and V, and from there, it will allow for the contents to be pasted without ruining the formatting, and it keeps the color, text, and font as well all in an even sense, and that is how it'll be seen in the document.

You can also highlight one areas of this, and you can choose what you think needs to be seen. To do this, you click once to put the text cursor in the area you want to highlight, and then hold shift, and from there, click the end of what you would like to highlight. This in turn will keep everything all nicely uniformed, making it look better than it did in the past.

With excel these days, you can actually add data bars to make it look better. You choose the data range that you would like to add, and from there, you go to home, and then conditional formatting, and then choose data bars. You can choose a color scheme that really creates an impactful look. This will in turn help to create a nice and much prettier look to your content.

Finally, let's talk designer, and this is actually a newer feature for powerpoint that makes your slides really stand out. While you're putting ideas onto the slide, designer actually works to help match the content in a way that creates professionally designed layouts, and you can integrate the pictures with text, and also helps to create charts, lists, and so much more, making it an even more and enhanced experience. You definitely can boost your powerpoint skills and presentations with everything that you do with this, making it even better.

With MS office, you can use it with the laptop and tablet of your choice, and all of these features added together create

Windows 10

a better, mo cohesive experience for you to have with your MS office devices.

Chapter 8—Tips and Tricks for Windows 10

Now that you have everything in place, you can now learn a few cool tips and tricks to help you really get the most out of Windows 10. It is a great system, and there is a lot that it can offer for you. Here, we'll discuss a few of the different facets that are available, and some tips and tricks you may not know.

Secret start menu

Do you like the start menu from the past, and you want to have a non-tiled experience? Well, you can have that, and it is kinda possible. To get this, you must right-click on the Windows icon within the bottom left, giving you a textural jump to a number of different destinations. You can then go to there in order to figure out what type of interface you want to have, and you can eliminate the need for those pesky tiles.

Adding the Desktop Button

The desktop button dates all the way back to Windows 7, but it is handy. In the bottom-right area of the desktop is a secret button. This is actually something a lot of people don't realize si there at the bottom and the right, beyond where the date and time are, and this small, invisible button allows you to minimize all of the Windows, and you can do this by hovering rather than clicking, and you can change this by fixing the peak to preview desktop function within the taskbar.

Cortana Tips

There is a lot that you can do with Cortana, and you can actually have her do a lot. You can tell Cortana to wake you up at a certain time, which is definitely helpful if you have a Windows smartphone utilized. You can also have Cortana give you weather reports too. It is pretty good and accurate, but you will want to make sure that you realize that the location services will be on, so remember that. There is also currency conversion too, which is pretty great, and it's an awesome feature especially if you're overseas. You can also have Cortana define words for you, and the system can also help you translate words too, which is pretty neat and helpful if you need something. You can pretty much ask Cortana anything, and while it doesn't have the smart home functions like Alexa, it does well at what it does. You can even get packages tracked with Cortana, and you can ask for updates on this based on the shipping numbers so that the assistant can figure it out for you.

File Explorer Sharing

File explorer also lets you share things as well. This is great if you have a file that you feel like you should share on social media. You choose the file, and then right-click, and then share, and you can then choose the recently contacted people, or apps that support sharing. Choose the apps that you want to share, and that's all there is to it. It's so simple, and yet so effective for sharing content.

Opening to This PC

This is a super helpful one, especially if you want to make sure that you access your PC, and have it access that rather than quick access. Quick access looks at most frequently used files and such, and while it's useful, you may want it to open this PC. To access that, go to file explorer, and right click quick access, selecting options, and from there, go to folder options, and the look for the label which indicates where to open file explorer to. You can then choose this PC, and then save, and exit it. It's that simple, but quite helpful if you definitely want to have an ease of use.

Shake it up

There is also the shake feature. It is pretty cool, because if you do have a display that's very cluttered, you grab the top of the window, shaking it to minimize all of the Windows. If you don't want to have them all go away, you simply shake it again to make it come back, which in turn will help you with improving how much you have on the screen, making the real estate much easier to deal with, and a much more effective system.

Slide to Shutdown

Finally, this is a trick that's only available in Windows 10. It is a bit complicated, and might only be possible if you are someone that wants to put the effort into this, but here, we'll discuss how you do this. You simply want to right-click on the desktop itself, and then go to new, and proceed to choose the option to shortcut. In the next popup menu, you want to put the system32/slidetoshutdown.exe in there, and from there, you should press enter. This will create a clickable icon within the desktop that you can rename. You then want to double click said icon in order to get a pull-down shade that's on there, and from there, it will be dragged all the way down to shut it down. It's a cool feature that you can use, but you should definitely be cautious, since this fully shuts the computer down, and it doens't create a sleep or hiberantion to it.

Windows 10

And there you have it, some cool tips, tricks, and features that you can get with Windows 10 that allow you to do so much with it, and in turn, help you improve the general state of use of this. Windows 10 is a great system that allows you to do much, and these tips and tricks will help you get started with this system and learning it.

Conclusion

As you can see, there is a lot to love here in terms of Windows 10. Microsoft has really made the operating system easier, more straightforward, cleaner, and better for users. It's perfect for both longtime fans and those who are relatively new.

There are many different features here, and many possibilities.

While you may not use all of these, learning to understand the different operating system settings is the best way to figure out what works for you. By using the tips in the previous chapters to help you create different shortcuts, pinning items to the taskbar, and the like, you can create your own personal ecosystem that makes it really easy for you to utilize.

Using Task View and Live Tile helps blend the classic look and functionality and integration of this. It can work on many other devices too, and if you have a tablet, you can use many of these settings for this as well. . even if you don't' like a feature for the tablet, it may be worth trying on a computer, so remember than when working to enhance your experience.

It can support many different devices, along with different peripherals, both made by Microsoft and third parties, so you definitely will want to see if you can link your devices to this as well.

The information here is enough to get you into this operating system, and if you do get curious and want to know more, know that there are different developers and techs that can help, and you can always go directly to Microsoft support and start a forum if you need help or have a question. You can always contact support too.

Windows 10 is the future, and knowing how to use this great system will help to improve your personal experience with it, making it better than before.

I hope, that you really enjoyed reading my book.

Thanks for buying the book anyway!

Made in the USA
Monee, IL
25 September 2019